SOCIOLOGY IN PRACTICE

OUR PRESCRIPTION FOR LIVING

FIRST

D1196824

WRITTEN AND EDITED BY TIMOTHY D. LEVONYAN RADLOFF

EAST STROUDSBURG UNIVERSITY

cognella® | ACADEMIC PUBLISHING

Bassim Hamadeh, CEO and Publisher
John Remington, Executive Editor
Gem Rabanera, Project Editor
Abbey Hastings, Associate Production Editor
Emely Villavicencio, Senior Graphic Designer
Trey Soto, Licensing Coordinator
Natalie Piccotti, Director of Marketing
Kassie Graves, Vice President of Editorial
Jamie Giganti, Director of Academic Publishing

ISBN: 978-1-5165-2858-5 (pbk) / 978-1-5165-2859-2 (br)

CONTENTS

PREFACE

The purpose of this book is to compliment the already existing introductory sociology texts that we use, not replace them. Introduction to Sociology is a course that provides a broad overview of the discipline, and its introductory textbooks usually introduce students to a wide variety of sociological concepts and theoretical perspectives that illustrate how sociologists apply them to better understand our social world. However, this supplementary reading takes it one step further by engaging students to think critically about how their personal lives are influenced by cultural and institutional forces.

Why take it one step further? Because sociologists argue that if we fail to grasp how the broader cultural and institutional forces impact our personal lives, then we will be unable to understand what happens to us in our personal lives. And even worse, as a result of not having knowledge of how the broader social forces affect our personal lives, we will not be able to make society better nor meet the demands of responsible citizenship.

Reflect for a moment on your own life, its successes and failures as well as all of its twists and turns. At some point during your reflection, you may begin to realize that the meaning of life and, more importantly, its challenges and tribulations are complex and extraordinary. How you got here to college, for example, just didn't happen or depend on you and your personal choices. Sociology teaches us that you were also influenced by our economy, your elementary and secondary education, your family, friends, and the community you were raised in. In other words, thinking sociologically shows you how you are connected to as well as influenced by larger social forces that affect not only the decisions that you make throughout your life, but also who you are as a person. And furthermore, as you attempt to make sense of who you are and where you are headed in your life, sociology reminds us that you must also take into account the life-changing societal events and trends such as the recent economic crisis including record levels of student loan debt, wars and terrorist attacks, high divorce rate, suicide, drug addiction, bullying, violence and mass shootings in our schools, communities, and workplaces. Therefore, it is my goal to engage students to think sociologically by providing them with the opportunity to reflect critically about how their own lives are impacted and shaped by cultural and institutional forces so that they can navigate their own life course more effectively through the most prevailing issues of our time.

ACKNOWLEDGMENTS

Thank you, Cognella! I am forever grateful to my project editor Gem Rabanera, as well as my associate production editor Abbey Hastings and developmental editor Susana Christie—for their assistance, support and guidance.

PART ONE

YOUR HIGHER EDUCATION SOCIOLOGICALLY REEXAMINED

College Graduates Face Social and Economic Crises

In Part 1, we will address the following topics:

- The social and economic challenges of the Millennial Generation in the 21st century.
- The American Dream and the meaning of higher education as an institutionalized norm.
- The role of higher education in the 21st century.
- Applying your sociological imagination to understand your employability as well as social responsibility in meeting the demands of responsible global citizenship.

Today, college graduates are facing social and economic crises that outpace any other college graduates in U.S. history. With record numbers of student loan debt, income stagnation, and high unemployment among today's college graduates, there is no doubt that people are questioning the value of not only earning a college degree, but also the validity of achieving the American Dream—i.e., working hard to earn financial independence leading ultimately to living more responsible and fulfilling lives. Indeed, there seems to be a general consensus among Americans that the younger adults ages 18 to 24 are facing more difficulties than their parents' generation (see Figure 1.1). For example, all of the adult respondents in a 2012 Pew Research study concerning social and economic trends pointed out that the basic necessities of achieving the American Dream—i.e., finding a job (82%), saving for the future (75%), paying for college (71%), and buying a home (69%)— are harder to accomplish than what their parents' generation had experienced some four to five decades ago (Pew Research Center, 2012).

FIGURE 1.1

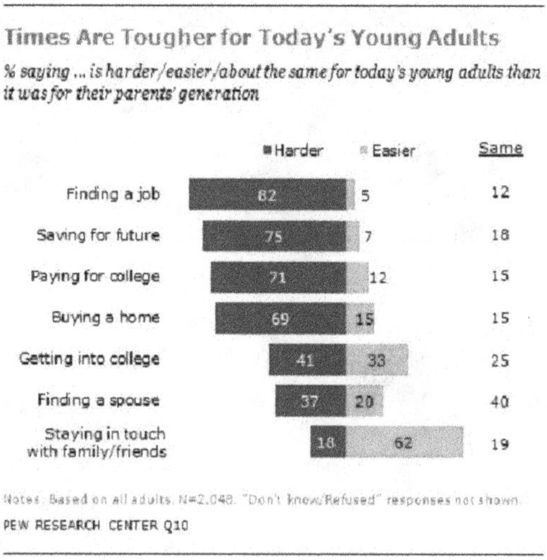

Times Are Tougher for Today's Young Adults

% saying ... is harder/easier/about the same for today's young adults than it was for their parents' generation

	Harder	Easier	Same
Finding a job	82	5	12
Saving for future	75	7	18
Paying for college	71	12	15
Buying a home	69	15	15
Getting into college	41	33	25
Finding a spouse	37	20	40
Staying in touch with family/friends	18	62	19

Notes: Based on all adults. N=2,048. "Don't know/Refused" responses not shown.
PEW RESEARCH CENTER Q10

SOURCE: Pew Research Center, "Times are Tougher for Today's Young Adults," http://www.pewsocialtrends.org/files/2012/02/young-underemployed-and-optimistic.pdf, pp. 22.

Furthermore, for most Americans, four to five decades ago, earning a college degree was not necessary in order to achieve the American Dream or a middle class lifestyle. In fact, America's post-World War II manufacturing economy was so prosperous in developing automobiles, medicine, weapons, and much more, that high school graduates were achieving the American Dream by entering into the workforce, earning decent wages, and learning the necessary skills on the job (Davidson, 2014). Furthermore, up until the early 20th century, very few Americans felt that the economy was a place for humans to reach their full potential. Rather, for most Americans back then, the economy was where one achieved personal fulfillment by earning financial success to acquire subsistence and material things (Hauhart, 2015). However, over the last thirty years or so, the American economy has shifted from a manufacturing to a service and more technologically advanced global economy; an economy where earning a four-year college degree has become a necessity for achieving the American Dream, or what sociologists call an *institutionalized norm**—i.e., earning a college degree and getting a job will bring financial success—to achieve at least a middle class lifestyle in the United States (Davidson, 2014; Newman, 2014). Indeed, economists have pointed out that the number of job opportunities that require some college education has more than doubled from 28% in 1973 to 59% in 2010, and is projected to increase to 65% by 2020 (Carnevale, Hanson, & Gulish, 2013).

Did you know...

... That almost two-thirds (61.9 percent) of college students said that they had "felt overwhelming anxiety" in the past 12 months in Fall 2016.
—American College Health Association Fall 2016 report

* **Institutionalized norm**: Expected patterns of behavior within a social institution.

And to be clear, even though having a college degree does not guarantee financial success in today's economy due to falling wages or wage stagnation and fewer job opportunities, college graduates still make more money, on average, than those who do not have a college degree (Cain Miller, 2014; Newman, 2014; Pew Research Center, 2014a). In addition, college graduates are more likely to believe that their education has prepared them for work and career advancement than those without any college education (Pew Research Center, 2014a). Lastly, the Centers for Disease Control and Prevention's (CDC) 2012 annual report had indicated that those with a college degree live longer and have healthier lives than those with only a high school education (CDC, 2012).

However, gone are the days where one can reach his or her full potential and achieve a middle class lifestyle simply by graduating from high school and then enter into the workforce to learn the necessary skills on the job. Today, the 21st century workforce expects college graduates to already have the requisite skills (acquired through postsecondary education and training) needed to meet the new demands of a more technologically advanced global society and economy (Carnevale, Hanson, & Gulish, 2013). Consequently, college students face increasing pressures to live up to the true meaning of the American Dream, as espoused by the American historian James Truslow Adams in 1931. In his book, *The Epic of America*, Adams was the first to coin the concept "the American Dream" to proclaim that every American should lead a much "richer and fuller" life by embracing the freedom and opportunity to work hard in accordance with one's human potential, not simply to achieve financial success to purchase material things (p. 317). In other words, the responsibility of personal fulfillment and success—i.e., achieving the American Dream—rests squarely on the shoulders of each individual to discover one's talents and abilities. Do you recognize the origin of Adams' individualistic ethos of personal responsibility and fulfillment? This way of thinking about ourselves (as Americans) can be traced back to the United States' founding document in the 18th century—The Declaration of Independence—declaring that each of us are created equal and provided "unalienable rights" by God to pursue our own happiness and life goals. As such, the moral fabric of our American individualistic culture is based on perceiving our own lives as the outcomes of individual accomplishments or failures as well as attributing other individual's accomplishments and failures to their abilities or personal qualities (Machum & Clow, 2015).

However, we see a generation, the Millennial Generation, not doing better than its parent's generation for the first time in American history. As of 2015, the Millennial Generation (ages 18-34) became the largest generation in the labor force (Pew Research Center 2015a). But, even so, the Millennial Generation has the highest unemployment rate at roughly 40% compared to its two predecessors—the Baby Boomers (23%) and Generation X (37%) (McGrath Goodman, 2015). Moreover, the Millennials in the labor force have experienced a significant decline in their annual earnings, change jobs more frequently (at least 6 times), and it now takes recent college graduates until age 30 (up from 26 since 1980) to reach the national median income (Carnevale, Hanson, & Gulish, 2013).

Consequently, as young women and men are experiencing severe hardships while trying to gain a foothold in today's global economy, research studies have linked their struggles and hardships to their mental and physical health—e.g., experiencing high blood pressure, anxiety, and depression, including thoughts of suicide, as well as feeling alienated and a growing distrust with the political and economic system (Abrams, 2014; Pew Research Center, 2014a). And even though a growing number of Millennials are questioning the validity of achieving the American Dream, they feel, for the most part, personally responsible for their own life circumstances in that achieving the American Dream rests squarely on their own shoulders (Machum & Clow, 2015; Silva, 2014).

Moreover, certain media messages blame the Millennials themselves for their lack of success and poor economic outcomes (Carnevale, Hanson, & Gulish, 2013; Silva, 2014). Many people are

FIGURE 1.2   MEDIA COVERAGE BLAMING THE MILLENNIALS.

Fig 1.2: Copyright © by Time Inc.

attacking the character of the Millennials as being irresponsible, lazy, and not having the necessary skills to make it in today's global economy (Carnevale, Hanson, & Gulish, 2013; see Figure 1.2). For example, the front cover of TIME magazine's May 2013 issue portrays a young woman who seems self-absorbed as she is posing to take an iPhone selfie. She appears to be doing what any normal young person would be doing on any given day. However, what's striking is how the headline as text—"The ME, ME, ME Generation: Millennials are lazy entitled narcissists ..."—is juxtaposed with her image thereby suggesting that her actions feed into the negative commentary that stereotype the Millennials as being self-obsessed with publicizing their lives while not caring about the world around them. As a result of already feeling alienated while at the same time embracing America's individualistic ethos, many Millennials are sinking deeper into their own personal troubles— i.e., one feels that his/her hardships or life challenges are a "private matter" involving their individual character and immediate relations with other people (Mills, 1959, p. 8).

Did you know ...

... That the Millennial Generation is the least likely to trust people in general.
—Pew Research Center 2014b

Over half a century ago, a very prominent sociologist by the name of C. Wright Mills (1916–1962) pointed out that as America was becoming more economically and militarily powerful, Americans felt trapped within their own personal troubles and were unable to "cope with the larger world with which they are [were] suddenly confronted" (quoted in Mills's, "The Promise," 1959, p. 6; and see third paragraph on p. 24 in the Reading 1.2 section). And as we fast forward to apply Mills's prescient sociological insights to present day's economic challenges, we see that due to America's individualistic culture, Millennials, like many Americans, are more likely to attribute their failures to personal characteristics—e.g., financial insecurity, incompetence, and low self-esteem—and as a result, overlook the broader cultural and institutional forces that are also responsible for their feelings of anxiety and alienation. In addition, levels of stress and anxiety are high for Millennials because they feel like they have no control over their lives. According to sociologists, one of the best prescriptions needed for reducing high levels of stress and anxiety, is to come to grips with how one's personal troubles are connected as well as influenced by "the public issues of social structure"—i.e., the historical, institutional, and cultural forces that transcend our personal lives (Mills, 1959, p. 8; and pages 28-29). In fact, Mills (1959) believed that through higher education and critical study of scientific knowledge, we can develop this "quality of mind" which he referred to as the *sociological imagination* (see page 25). In simple terms, applying your sociological imagination means to reflect critically about how your personal lives are influenced and shaped by large-scale societal forces including history, culture, economic, and political factors.

Sociology teaches us that society is a human creation made up of interrelated parts that work together to provide meaning, purpose, structure, and organization in our everyday lives. Metaphorically speaking, imagine society's interrelated parts as "pieces of the puzzle" where each piece helps us understand how our "self" is interconnected with larger societal forces. Consider these "pieces of the puzzle" as building blocks of society that help us understand how our interpersonal, cultural, and institutional activities are patterned within society:

1. <u>Statuses</u>—socio-culturally defined positions individuals occupy within society.

   ☐ *Roles* → set of expectations (obligations and duties) associated with a particular status.
   ✓ *Ascribed*—sociocultural position acquired at birth or entered involuntarily later in life (e.g., race, sex, and ethnicity).
   ✓ *Achieved*—sociocultural position taken on voluntarily or acquired through effort or action (e.g., college student, employee, or parent).

2. <u>Groups</u>—interaction involving at least two people who are conscious of their group identity.

   ☐ Types of groups →
   ✓ *Primary*—small, close ties, and have an emotional attachment (e.g., family and close friends).
   ✓ *Secondary*—formal, impersonal, and established to perform specific tasks (e.g., co-workers and classmates).
   ✓ *In-group*—strongly identify with one another, and have a great sense of loyalty.
   ✓ *Out-group*—outcast, and looked down upon.

3. <u>Organizations</u>—networks of statuses & groups created for a specific purpose.

   ☐ Types of organizations →
   ✓ Religious (e.g., church, synagogue, mosque, etc.).
   ✓ Economic (e.g., Wall Street, Microsoft, General Motors, World Bank, etc.).
   ✓ Political (e.g., political parties, political action committees, etc.).
   ✓ Educational (e.g., elementary, secondary, and postsecondary).
   ✓ Medical (e.g., hospitals, clinics, etc.).
   ✓ Military defense (e.g., Army, Air Force, Marines, Navy, etc.).

4. <u>Social institutions</u>—make up the foundation of society as the building blocks that organize society to meet peoples' needs.

   ◻ Examples of social institutions →
   ✓ *Family*—essential for identity, sense of belonging, reproduction, and training of morals.
   ✓ *Education*—to provide knowledge, train for future profession/careers, and teach what it means to be a productive member of society.
   ✓ *Economy*—to ensure that societies have systematic ways of gathering resources, converting them into goods and commodities, and distributing them to people.
   ✓ *Politics & law*—to preserve order, protect citizens, and enforce and create laws.
   ✓ *Mass media*—coverage of local, national, and international current events to inform the public; shapes and molds public opinion.
   ✓ *Health care*—serves to heal the sick and prevent sickness and disease by prescribing medical treatments using science and technology.
   ✓ *Military*—serves to protect citizens from both domestic and international threats.
   ✓ *Religion*—provides a spiritual interpretation of existence as well as a moral foundation.

5. <u>Culture</u>—the mortar that holds all of these "pieces of the puzzle" together.

   ◻ Shared beliefs and values →
   ✓ Provide us with codes of conduct—proper and acceptable ways of doing things. We share common beliefs and values because of culture.

To further illustrate how to apply your sociological imagination or to think sociologically, check out the Thinking Sociologically (Reading 1.1) section below.

Reading 1.1
Thinking Sociologically

Steven M. Buechler

The sociological perspective involves several themes. They overlap with one another, and some may be found in other social sciences as well as everyday consciousness. Taken together, they comprise a distinctive lens for viewing the social world. Here are some of those themes.

Society is a Social Construction

People construct social order. Sociology does not see society as God-given, as biologically determined, or as following any predetermined plan beyond human intervention. At the same time, this does not mean that everyone plays an equal role in the process or that the final product looks like what people intended.

Social construction begins with intentions that motivate people to act in certain ways. When many people have similar goals and act in concert, larger social patterns or institutions are created. Goal-driven action is essential to the creation of institutions, and it remains equally important to their maintenance and transformation over time. Put succinctly, society is a human product (Berger and Luckmann 1966).

Basic human needs ensure some similarities in the goals that people pursue in all times and places. But these pursuits also unfold in specific historical circumstances

Steven M. Buechler, Selection from "How to Think Sociologically," *Critical Sociology*, pp. 6-12, 281-290. Copyright © 2014 by Taylor & Francis Group. Reprinted with permission.

and cultural contexts that have led to a dazzling variety of social worlds. This variety is itself the best evidence of the socially constructed nature of social worlds. If biology or genetics were the determining force behind social worlds, wouldn't they look a lot more similar than what we actually see around the globe?

Social constructionists thus insist that society arises from the goal-driven action of people. But they also recognize that the institutions created by such actions take on a life of their own. They appear to exist independently of the people who create and sustain them. They are experienced by people as a powerful external force that weighs down on them. When this external force becomes severe enough, people are likely to lose sight of the fact that society is a social product in the first place.

The value of the social constructionist premise is this dual recognition. On one hand, society is a subjective reality originating in the intentions of social actors. On the other hand, it becomes an objective reality that confronts subsequent generations as a social fact that inevitably shapes *their* intentional actions—and so it goes. Understood this way, the idea that society is a social construction is at the heart of the sociological perspective.

Society Is an Emergent Reality

Another premise of sociology is emergentism. This reveals sociology's distinctive level of analysis. For psychology, the level of analysis is the individual, even if it is acknowledged that individuals belong to groups. For sociology, the level of analysis is social ties rather than individual elements. Emergentism recognizes that certain realities only appear when individual elements are combined in particular ways. When they are, qualitatively new realities emerge through these combinations.

Take a simple example. Imagine a random pile of ten paper clips. Now imagine linking these paper clips together to form a chain. There are still ten paper clips, but a new emergent reality has appeared that is qualitatively different from the random pile because of how the elements are related to one another. Or consider human reproduction. Neither sperm nor egg is capable of producing human life on its own; in combination, qualitatively new life begins to emerge from a particular combination of elements.

Sociology specializes in the social level of analysis that emerges when elements are combined to create new, larger realities. Emergentism also implies that when we try to understand elements outside of their context, it is at best a simplification and at worst a distortion. The parts derive meaning from their relationship with other parts, and the sociological perspective is fundamentally attuned to such relationships.

Society Is a Historical Product

Thinking historically is a crucial part of the sociological imagination (Mills 1959). Classical sociologists thought historically because they lived in times of rapid social change and it was a major challenge to understand such change. Modern sociology tends to be more static, and modern people tend to be very present-oriented. Both professional and practical sociologists would benefit from a more historical perspective on the social world.

Seeing society as a historical product means recognizing that we cannot understand the present without understanding the past. Historical knowledge of past social conditions provides crucial comparisons. Without such benchmarks, it is impossible to understand what is genuinely new in the present day. Without a historical referent for comparison, sociology is clueless when it comes to understanding social change. Historical knowledge also provides the raw material for categories, comparisons, typologies, and analogies that are crucial to understanding both the present and possible future worlds.

The concept of emergentism applies here because the importance of seeing relationships between elements also works chronologically. If we look at society at only one point in time, we sever it from its past and its potential futures. Its very meaning arises from these relationships; to ignore them is to distort even the static understanding of society at one point in time. Consider the difference between a photograph and a film that presents a succession of images. We can learn something from the still photo, but its meaning often changes dramatically when we see it as one of a series of interrelated images.

Society Consists of Social Structures

Sociologists use the term *structure* to refer to the emergent products of individual elements. Structure implies that the social world has certain patterns or regularities that recur over time. Put differently, sociologists are keenly interested in social organization.

Structures are products of human purposes, but they acquire an objective reality and become a powerful influence on human action. Think about how physical structures like buildings shape action. We almost always enter buildings through doors; in rare cases we might do so through windows, but walking through walls is not an option. Social structures are less visible and more flexible than buildings, but they also channel people's actions, because they make some actions routine and expected, others possible but unlikely, and still others all but impossible.

Like buildings, social structures often have a vertical dimension. Social structures ensure that some people are better off than others and that some are not very well off at all. Some residential buildings have penthouses at the top, premium suites near the top, standard accommodations below them, and housekeeping staff in the basement. Social structures are also stratified, granting power, privilege, and opportunity to some while limiting or denying them to others. Sociologists are especially interested in the hierarchical dimension of social structures.

Sociologists traditionally thought of social structures as powerful forces weighing down upon the individual. In this image, structures constrain freedom of choice and behavior. But this is a one-sided view. Structures are constraining, but they are also enabling. These established patterns of social organization also make many actions possible in the first place or easier in the second place. Without pre-existing social structures, we would have to do everything "from scratch," and the challenge of sheer survival might overwhelm us. The trick is thus to see social structures as simultaneously constraining and enabling social action (Giddens 1984).

Society Consists of Reflexive Actors

People in society are aware of themselves, of others, and of their relationships with others. As reflexive actors, we monitor our action and its effects on others. We continue, modify, or halt actions, depending on whether they are achieving their intended effects. According to one school of thought, we are literally actors, because social life is like a theatrical performance in which we try to convince others that we are a certain kind of person (Goffman 1959). To stage effective performances, we must constantly be our own critic, judging and refining our performances. Reflexivity thus means that when we act, we are conscious of our action, we monitor its course, and we make adjustments over time.

To stage such performances, we must undergo socialization. Along the way, we acquire a language that provides us with tools for reflexive thinking. We also acquire a self. Oddly enough, to have a self requires that we first have relationships with others. Through those relationships, we imaginatively see the world from their perspective, which includes seeing ourselves as we imagine we appear to them. It is this ability to see ourselves through the perspective of others—to see ourselves as an object—that defines the self. Reflexive action only becomes possible with a self.

Reflexivity makes ordinary people into practical sociologists. To be a competent person is to be a practical sociologist. We cannot help being sociologists every time we ponder a potential relationship, reconsider a hasty action, or adopt someone else's viewpoint. All such situations call upon and refine the reflexivity that is the hallmark of social action as well as a defining characteristic of the sociological perspective.

Society Is an Interaction of Agency and Structure

Social structures and reflexive actors are intimately connected. Unfortunately, much sociology emphasizes one side of this connection at the expense of the other. Agency centered views stress the ability of people to make choices out of a range of alternatives in almost any situation. The emphasis on choice implies that people control their own destiny, at least within broad limits. Structure-centered views stress the extent to which people's choices are limited by social structures. The emphasis on structures implies that people's options—if not their lives—are essentially determined by larger social forces over which they have little control. Both approaches have merit, but the challenge is to see structure and agency in a more interconnected way.

Marx once said that people make their own history (acknowledging agency), but under circumstances they do not choose but rather inherit from the past (acknowledging structure). Here's an analogy from the game of pool. Each time you approach the table, you "inherit" a structure left by your opponent when they missed their last shot. Yet, for every layout of balls on the table, there is always a shot that you can attempt, and that action will alter the structure of the table for subsequent shots. In this analogy, structure (the position of balls on the table) both limits and creates opportunities for agency (taking a shot), which in turn alters the structure for the next round of shooting. If pool is not your game, chess is also a good analogy. The point is that agency and structure are two sides of the same coin; each conditions the possibilities of the other as we make our own history in circumstances we don't choose.

The close connection between structure and agency has led one theorist to reject the notion of structure altogether, because it implies something that exists apart from agency. Anthony Giddens (1984) talks about a *process* of structuration. In this view, actors use preexisting structures to accomplish their goals, but they also re-create them as a by-product of their actions. Consider a wedding ceremony. It is a preexisting cultural ritual people use to accomplish the goal of getting married. The by-product of all these individual marriages is the perpetuation of the cultural ritual itself. Generalize this to any situation in which we draw upon an established part of our social world to achieve a goal; in using this part we also sustain (and perhaps transform) it as a part of social structure.

Society Has Multiple Levels

Although society has multiple levels, sociologists often focus on one level at a time. Think about using Google Maps to locate a destination. You can zoom out to get the big picture at the expense of not seeing some important details. Alternatively, you can zoom in on some key details at the expense of not seeing the big picture. Combining these differing views will orient you to your destination, but we must remember it is ultimately all one interconnected landscape.

Sociologists nevertheless distinguish between macro and micro levels of society. When we look at the macro level, we typically include millions of people organized into large categories, groups, or institutions. The macro level is the "big picture" or "high altitude" perspective in which society's largest patterns are evident and individuals are invisible. When we look at the micro level, we might inspect no more than a dozen people interacting in a small group setting. Here, the role of particular individuals is very prominent, and larger social patterns fade into the background.

Some of the best sociology involves understanding not only structure-agency connections but also micro-macro links. Every macro-structure rests on micro-interaction, and every micro-interaction is shaped by macro-structures. The previous example of a wedding also illustrates this point. On the macro level, weddings are a cultural ritual that inducts people into the institution of marriage and the family. However, weddings, marriage, and the family would not exist on the macro level without countless, micro-level interactions. The macro-level institution depends on micro-level actions to sustain it. At the same time, anyone who has ever gotten married will tell you that macro-level, cultural expectations about weddings impose themselves on people as they plan for this supposedly personal event. Every micro-level wedding depends on a macro-level, cultural blueprint for its social significance. The micro and macro levels of society are one interdependent reality rather than two separate things.

Society Involves Unintended Consequences

One of the more profound insights of the sociological perspective concerns unintended and unanticipated consequences of action. Much human action is purposive or goal-directed. People act because they want to accomplish something. Despite this, they sometimes fail to achieve their goals. But whether people achieve their goals or not, their actions always create other consequences that they don't intend or even anticipate. Shakespeare made a profoundly sociological point when he had Juliet fake her own suicide to dramatize her love for Romeo. Unfortunately, the plan never reached Romeo. Juliet neither intended nor anticipated that Romeo would find her unconscious, believe that she was really dead, and take his own life in response. Nor did he intend (or even realize) that she would awaken, discover his real death, and really take her life in response. Talk about unintended consequences!

This principle acknowledges the complexity of the social world and the limits on our ability to control it. It says that despite our best efforts, the effects of social action cannot be confined to one intended path; they always spill over into unexpected areas. The principle is also a cautionary message for those seeking to solve social problems. Such efforts might succeed, but they often bring other consequences that are neither positive nor intended.

Efforts to control crime provide an example. Consider policies to "get tough" on crime through harsher treatment like capital punishment and mandatory sentencing. Because the human beings who serve as judges and juries are reflexive actors who take these facts into account, they are often less likely to convict suspects without overwhelming evidence because of the harshness of the sentence. Thus, the unintended consequence of an attempt to "get tough" on crime might be the opposite, because fewer suspects are convicted than before.

A related idea is the distinction between manifest and latent functions. A manifest function is an outcome that people intend. A latent function is an outcome that people are not aware of; it can complement, but it often contradicts, the manifest function. Crime and punishment provide yet another example. The manifest function of imprisonment is punishment or rehabilitation. The latent function is to bring criminals together where they can meet one another, exchange crime techniques, and become better criminals upon their return to society.

The concept of latent functions is crucial to sociological analysis. Sometimes we observe behavior or rituals that seem irrational, pointless, or self-defeating. This is the time to begin looking for latent functions. What we will often find is that such "irrational" behavior reinforces the identity and sustains the cohesion of the group that performs it. Thus, before we dismiss the tribal rain dance (because "rain gods" don't exist), we must explore its latent function. Even when people don't (manifestly) know what they are (latently) doing, their behavior can be crucial to group cohesion.

Recognizing unintended consequences and latent functions is not just for professional sociologists. Daily living requires managing risk, and ordinary people in everyday life recognize the tricky nature of goal-directed action. The folk wisdom that "the road to hell is paved with good intentions" acknowledges the potential disconnect between goals and outcomes. Such recognition, however, never completely prevents outcomes we neither intend nor expect. These principles give social life some of its most surprising twists, and sociology some of its most fascinating challenges.

No attempt to capture the sociological perspective in a small number of themes can be complete. Other sociologists would doubtless modify this list. But most would recognize these themes as central to thinking sociologically. As such, they provide a foundation for the more detailed investigations to follow.

References

Berger, Peter, and Thomas Luckmann. 1966. *The Social Construction of Reality*. Garden City, NY: Anchor.

Giddens, Anthony. 1984. *The Constitution of Society*. Berkeley: University of California Press.

Goffman, Erving. 1959. *The Presentation of Self in Everyday Life*. Garden City, NY: Anchor

Mills, C. Wright. 1959. *The Sociological Imagination*. New York: Oxford University Press.

Sociology's promise is not only to engage you to develop a critical understanding (sociological understanding) of the world you live in and your place in it, but also empower you to become more active and responsible global citizens. Employing your sociological imagination means to challenge your own commonly held assumptions about personal troubles (private matters) like depression, anxiety, alienation, suicide, drug addiction, divorce or family disruption, domestic violence, eating disorders, sexist and racist ideologies, financial insecurity, and unemployment. In other words, critically examine how these seemingly private matters also arise due to cultural and institutional forces in order to gain deeper sociological insights into how our self is interconnected to the world we live in. Furthermore, developing deeper sociological insights can help guide us to see that our personal troubles cannot be solved by solely changing our own personal characteristics or individual attributes, but also by transforming the culture, institutions, and organizations that impact us all as well. Inspired by C. Wright Mills's three sociological questions found on page 27 in 'The Promise' section that follows, I provide you with a sociological framework within which to identify those social mechanisms that link our own personal lives with large-scale societal forces. By identifying those social mechanisms, you will gain the ability to navigate not only your transition from college to the "real world" more effectively, but also through the most prevailing issues we face in the 21st century. Our sociological framework engages you to apply the following sociological questions to your own life:

1. How are activities patterned in our society? Our particular focus here is to examine how your social psychological circumstances (personal troubles)—i.e., identify what you think and feel about your life challenges as well as developing a meaningful life—are connected with the purpose and functioning of social institutions—e.g., family, education, economy (workplace), law and politics and culture—(public issues of social structure). Critically reflect on how your own ascribed and achieved statuses are influenced and shaped by these public issues of social structure.

2. Where is society located in its history? Most importantly, critically examine the progress we have made over the last 70 years or so since World War II. Focus your attention particularly on how the social institutions, especially the economy, and culture functioned in the past versus how they are functioning presently with respect to improving the quality of your life.

3. What kinds of people are produced in society? Ask yourself, do you feel concerned about your future in terms of the value of your education, future employment prospects, and quality of life. Are the social institutions and culture providing you with opportunities to reach your fullest potential as well as preparing you to meet the demands of responsible global citizenship?

Reading 1.2
The Promise

C. Wright Mills

Nowadays men often feel that their private lives are a series of traps. They sense that within their everyday worlds, they cannot overcome their troubles, and in this feeling, they are often quite correct: What ordinary men are directly aware of and what they try to do are bounded by the private orbits in which they live; their visions and their powers are limited to the close-up scenes of job, family, neighborhood; in other milieux, they move vicariously and remain spectators. And the more aware they become, however vaguely, of ambitions and of threats which transcend their immediate locales, the more trapped they seem to feel.

Underlying this sense of being trapped are seemingly impersonal changes in the very structure of continent-wide societies. The facts of contemporary history are also facts about the success and the failure of individual men and women. When a society is industrialized, a peasant becomes a worker; a feudal lord is liquidated or becomes a businessman. When classes rise or fall, a man is employed or unemployed; when the rate of investment goes up or down, a man takes new heart or goes broke. When wars happen, an insurance salesman becomes a rocket launcher; a store clerk, a radar man; a wife lives alone; a child grows up without a father. Neither the life of an individual nor the history of a society can be understood without understanding both.

Yet men do not usually define the troubles they endure in terms of historical change and institutional contradiction. The well-being they enjoy, they do not usually impute to the big ups and downs of the societies in which they live. Seldom aware of the intricate connection between the patterns of their own lives and the course of world history, ordinary men do not usually know what this connection means for the kinds of men they are becoming and for the kinds of history-making in which they might take part. They do not possess the quality of mind essential to grasp the interplay of man and society, of biography and history, of self and world. They cannot cope with their personal troubles in such ways as to control the structural transformations that usually lie behind them.

Surely it is no wonder. In what period have so many men been so totally exposed at so fast a pace to such earthquakes of change? That Americans have not known such catastrophic changes as have the men and women of other societies is due to historical facts that are now quickly becoming 'merely history.' The history that now affects every man is world history. Within this scene and this period, in the course of a single generation, one sixth of mankind is transformed from all that is feudal and backward into all that is modern, advanced, and fearful. Political colonies are freed; new and less visible forms of imperialism installed. Revolutions occur; men feel the intimate grip of new kinds of authority. Totalitarian societies rise, and are smashed to bits—or succeed fabulously. After two centuries of ascendancy, capitalism is shown up as only one way to make society into an industrial apparatus. After two centuries of hope, even formal democracy is restricted to a quite small portion of mankind. Everywhere in the underdeveloped world, ancient ways of life are broken up and vague expectations become urgent demands. Everywhere in the overdeveloped world, the means of authority and of violence become total in scope and bureaucratic in form. Humanity itself now lies before us, the super-nation at either pole concentrating its most coordinated and massive efforts upon the preparation of World War Three.

The very shaping of history now outpaces the ability of men to orient themselves in accordance with cherished values. And which values? Even when they do not panic, men often sense that older ways of feeling and thinking have collapsed and that newer beginnings are ambiguous to the point of moral stasis. Is it any wonder that ordinary men feel they cannot cope with the larger worlds with which they are so suddenly confronted? That they cannot understand the meaning of their epoch for their own lives? That—in defense of selfhood—they become morally insensible, trying to remain altogether private men? Is it any wonder that they come to be possessed by a sense of the trap?

It is not only information that they need—in this Age of Fact, information often dominates their attention and overwhelms their capacities to assimilate it. It is not only the skills of reason that they need—although their struggles to acquire these often exhaust their limited moral energy.

What they need, and what they feel they need, is a quality of mind that will help them to use information and to develop reason in order to achieve lucid summations of what is going on in the world and of what may be happening within themselves. It is this quality, I am going to contend, that journalists and scholars, artists and publics, scientists and editors are coming to expect of what may be called the sociological imagination.

1

The sociological imagination enables its possessor to understand the larger historical scene in terms of its meaning for the inner life and the external career of a variety of individuals. It enables him to take into account how individuals, in the welter of their daily experience, often become falsely conscious of their social positions. Within that welter, the framework of modern society is sought, and within that framework the psychologies of a variety of men and women are formulated. By such means the personal uneasiness of individuals is focused upon explicit troubles and the indifference of publics is transformed into involvement with public issues.

The first fruit of this imagination—and the first lesson of the social science that embodies it—is the idea that the individual can understand his own experience and gauge his own fate only by locating himself within his period, that he can know his own chances in life only by becoming aware of those of all individuals in his circumstances. In many ways it is a terrible lesson; in many ways a magnificent one. We do not know the limits of man's capacities for supreme effort or willing degradation, for agony or glee, for pleasurable brutality or the sweetness of reason. But in our time we have come to know that the limits of 'human nature' are frighteningly broad. We have come to know that every individual lives, from one generation to the next, in some society; that he lives out a biography, and that he lives it out within some historical sequence. By the fact of his living he contributes, however minutely, to the shaping of this society and to the course of its history, even as he is made by society and by its historical push and shove.

The sociological imagination enables us to grasp history and biography and the relations between the two within society. That is its task and its promise. To recognize this task and this promise is the mark of the classic social analyst. It is characteristic of Herbert Spencer—turgid, polysyllabic, comprehensive; of E. A. Ross—graceful, muckraking, upright; of Auguste Comte and Emile Durkheim; of the intricate and subtle Karl Mannheim. It is the quality of all that is intellectually excellent in Karl Marx; it is the clue to Thorstein Veblen's brilliant and ironic insight, to Joseph Schumpeter's many-sided constructions of reality; it is the basis of the psychological sweep of W. E. H. Lecky no less than of the profundity and clarity of Max Weber. And it is the signal of what is best in contemporary studies of man and society.

No social study that does not come back to the problems of biography, of history and of their intersections within a society has completed its intellectual journey. Whatever the specific problems of the classic social analysts, however limited or however broad the features of social reality they have examined, those who have been imaginatively aware of the promise of their work have consistently asked three sorts of questions:

1. What is the structure of this particular society as a whole? What are its essential components, and how are they related to one another? How does it differ from other varieties of social order? Within it, what is the meaning of any particular feature for its continuance and for its change?

2. Where does this society stand in human history? What are the mechanics by which it is changing? What is its place within and its meaning for the development of humanity as a whole? How does any particular feature we are examining affect, and how is it affected by, the historical period in which it moves? And this period— what are its essential features? How does it differ from other periods? What are its characteristic ways of history-making?

3. What varieties of men and women now prevail in this society and in this period? And what varieties are coming to prevail? In what ways are they selected and formed, liberated and repressed, made sensitive and blunted? What kinds of 'human nature' are revealed in the conduct and character we observe in this society in this period? And what is the meaning for 'human nature' of each and every feature of the society we are examining?

Whether the point of interest is a great power state or a minor literary mood, a family, a prison, a creed—these are the kinds of questions the best social analysts have asked. They are the intellectual pivots of classic studies of man in society—and they are the questions inevitably raised by any mind possessing the sociological imagination. For that imagination is the capacity to shift from one perspective to another—from the political to the psychological; from examination of a single family to comparative assessment of the national budgets of the world; from the theological school to the military establishment; from considerations of an oil industry to studies of contemporary poetry. It is the capacity to range from the most impersonal and remote transformations to the most intimate features of the human self—and to see the relations between the two. Back of its use there is always the urge to know the social and historical meaning of the individual in the society and in the period in which he has his quality and his being.

That, in brief, is why it is by means of the sociological imagination that men now hope to grasp what is going on in the world, and to understand what is happening in themselves as minute points of the intersections of biography and history within society. In large part, contemporary man's self-conscious view of himself as at least an outsider, if not a permanent stranger, rests upon an absorbed realization of social relativity and of the transformative power of history. The sociological imagination is the most fruitful form of this self-consciousness. By its use men whose mentalities have swept only a series of limited orbits often come to feel as if suddenly awakened in a house with which they had only supposed themselves to be familiar. Correctly or incorrectly, they often come to feel that they can now provide themselves with adequate summations, cohesive assessments, comprehensive orientations. Older decisions that once appeared sound now seem to them products of a mind unaccountably dense. Their capacity for astonishment is made lively again. They acquire a new way of thinking, they experience a transvaluation of values: in a word, by their reflection and by their sensibility, they realize the cultural meaning of the social sciences.

2

Perhaps the most fruitful distinction with which the sociological imagination works is between 'the personal troubles of milieu' and 'the public issues of social structure.' This distinction is an essential tool of the sociological imagination and a feature of all classic work in social science.

Troubles occur within the character of the individual and within the range of his immediate relations with others; they have to do with his self and with those limited areas of social life of which he is directly and personally aware. Accordingly, the statement and the resolution of troubles properly lie within the individual as a biographical entity and within the scope of his immediate milieu—the social setting that is directly open to his personal experience and to some extent his willful activity. A trouble is a private matter: values cherished by an individual are felt by him to be threatened.

Issues have to do with matters that transcend these local environments of the individual and the range of his inner life. They have to do with the organization of many such milieux into the institutions of an historical society as a whole, with the ways in which various milieux overlap and interpenetrate to form the larger structure of social and historical life. An issue is a public matter: some value cherished by publics is felt to be threatened. Often there is a debate about what that value really is and about what it is that really threatens it. This debate is often without focus if only because it is the very nature of an issue, unlike even widespread trouble, that it cannot very well be defined in terms of the immediate and everyday environments of ordinary men. An issue, in fact, often involves a crisis in institutional arrangements, and often too it involves what Marxists call 'contradictions' or 'antagonisms.'

In these terms, consider unemployment. When, in a city of 100,000, only one man is unemployed, that is his personal trouble, and for its relief we properly look to the character of the man, his skills, and his immediate opportunities. But when in a nation of 50 million employees, 15 million men are unemployed, that is an issue, and we may not hope to find its solution within the range of opportunities open to any one individual. The very structure of opportunities has collapsed. Both the correct statement of the problem and the range of possible solutions require us to consider the economic and political institutions of the society, and not merely the personal situation and character of a scatter of individuals.

Consider war. The personal problem of war, when it occurs, may be how to survive it or how to die in it with honor; how to make money out of it; how to climb into the higher safety of the military apparatus; or how to contribute to the war's termination. In short, according to one's values, to find a set of milieux and within it to survive the war or make one's death in it meaningful. But the structural issues of war have to do with its causes; with what types of men it throws up into command; with its effects upon economic and political, family and religious institutions, with the unorganized irresponsibility of a world of nation-states.

Consider marriage. Inside a marriage a man and a woman may experience personal troubles, but when the divorce rate during the first four years of marriage is 250 out of every 1,000 attempts, this is an indication of a structural issue having to do with the institutions of marriage and the family and other institutions that bear upon them.

Or consider the metropolis—the horrible, beautiful, ugly, magnificent sprawl of the great city. For many upper-class people, the personal solution to 'the problem of the city' is to have an apartment with private garage under it in the heart of the city, and forty miles out, a house by Henry Hill, garden by Garrett Eckbo, on a hundred acres of private land. In these two controlled environments—with a small staff at each end and a private helicopter connection—most people could solve many of the problems of personal milieux caused by the facts of the city. But all this, however splendid, does not solve the public issues that the structural fact of the city poses. What should be done with this wonderful monstrosity? Break it all up into scattered units, combining residence and work? Refurbish it as it stands? Or, after evacuation, dynamite it and build new cities according to new plans in new places? What should those plans be? And who is to decide and to accomplish whatever choice is made? These are structural issues; to confront them and to solve them requires us to consider political and economic issues that affect innumerable milieux.

In so far as an economy is so arranged that slumps occur, the problem of unemployment becomes incapable of personal solution. In so far as war is inherent in the nation-state system and in the uneven industrialization of the world, the ordinary individual in his restricted milieu will be powerless—with or without psychiatric aid—to solve the troubles this system or lack of system imposes upon him. In so far as the family as an institution turns women into darling little slaves and men into their chief providers and unweaned dependents, the problem of a satisfactory marriage remains incapable of purely private solution. In so far as the overdeveloped megalopolis and the overdeveloped automobile are built-in features of the overdeveloped society, the issues of urban living will not be solved by personal ingenuity and private wealth.

What we experience in various and specific milieux, I have noted, is often caused by structural changes. Accordingly, to understand the changes of many personal milieux we are required to look beyond them. And the number and variety of such structural changes increase as the institutions within which we live become more embracing and more intricately connected with one another. To be aware of the idea of social structure and to use it with sensibility is to be capable of tracing such linkages among a great variety of milieux. To be able to do that is to possess the sociological imagination.

3

What are the major issues for publics and the key troubles of private individuals in our time? To formulate issues and troubles, we must ask what values are cherished yet threatened, and what values are cherished and supported, by the characterizing trends of our period. In the case both of threat and of support we must ask what salient contradictions of structure may be involved.

When people cherish some set of values and do not feel any threat to them, they experience *well-being*. When they cherish values but *do* feel them to be threatened, they experience a crisis—either as a personal trouble or as a public issue. And if all their values seem involved, they feel the total threat of panic.

But suppose people are neither aware of any cherished values nor experience any threat? That is the experience of *indifference*, which, if it seems to involve all their values, becomes apathy. Suppose, finally, they are unaware of any cherished values, but still are very much aware of a threat? That is the experience of *uneasiness*, of anxiety, which, if it is total enough, becomes a deadly unspecified malaise.

Ours is a time of uneasiness and indifference—not yet formulated in such ways as to permit the work of reason and the play of sensibility. Instead of troubles—defined in terms of values and threats—there is often the misery of vague uneasiness; instead of explicit issues there is often merely the beat feeling that all is somehow not right. Neither the values threatened nor whatever threatens them has been stated; in short, they have not been carried to the point of decision. Much less have they been formulated as problems of social science.

In the 'thirties there was little doubt—except among certain deluded business circles that there was an economic issue which was also a pack of personal troubles. In these arguments about 'the crisis of capitalism,' the formulations of Marx and the many unacknowledged re-formulations of his work probably set the leading terms of the issue, and some men came to understand their personal troubles in these terms. The values threatened were plain to see and cherished by all; the structural contradictions that threatened them also seemed plain. Both were widely and deeply experienced. It was a political age.

But the values threatened in the era after World War Two are often neither widely acknowledged as values nor widely felt to be threatened. Much private uneasiness goes unformulated; much public malaise and many decisions of enormous structural relevance never become public issues. For those who accept such inherited values as reason and freedom, it is the uneasiness itself that is the trouble; it is the indifference itself that is the issue. And it is this condition, of uneasiness and indifference, that is the signal feature of our period.

All this is so striking that it is often interpreted by observers as a shift in the very kinds of problems that need now to be formulated. We are frequently told that the problems of our decade, or even the crises of our period, have shifted from the external realm of economics and now have to do with the quality of individual life—in fact with the question of whether there is soon going to be anything that can properly be called individual life. Not child labor but comic books, not poverty but mass leisure, are at the center of concern. Many great public issues as well as many private troubles are described in terms of 'the psychiatric'—often, it seems, in a pathetic attempt to avoid the large issues and problems of modern society. Often this statement seems to rest upon a provincial narrowing of interest to the Western societies, or even to the United States—thus ignoring two-thirds of mankind; often, too, it arbitrarily divorces the individual life from the larger institutions within which that life is enacted, and which on occasion bear upon it more grievously than do the intimate environments of childhood.

Problems of leisure, for example, cannot even be stated without considering problems of work. Family troubles over comic books cannot be formulated as problems without considering the plight of the contemporary family in its new relations with the newer institutions of the social structure. Neither leisure nor its debilitating uses can be understood as problems without recognition of the extent to which malaise and indifference now form the social and personal climate of contemporary American society. In this climate, no problems of 'the private life' can be stated and solved without recognition of the crisis of ambition that is part of the very career of men at work in the incorporated economy.

It is true, as psychoanalysts continually point out, that people do often have 'the increasing sense of being moved by obscure forces within themselves which they are unable to define.' But it is *not* true, as Ernest Jones asserted, that 'man's chief enemy and danger is his own unruly nature and the dark forces pent up within him.' On the contrary: 'Man's chief danger' today lies in the unruly forces of contemporary society itself, with its alienating methods of production, its enveloping techniques of political domination, its international anarchy—in a word, its pervasive transformations of the very 'nature' of man and the conditions and aims of his life.

Developing a Sociological Understanding of the Role of Higher Education

Have you ever asked yourself why you are here seeking a four-year college degree? Is it merely to better your skills and to improve your knowledge in order to be competitive in the job market so that you can get a good quality paying job? After all, we are taught that having a good quality job and earning money are necessary in order to achieve financial stability, happiness, and success in our lives. But is that all you need? Is life only about getting the best occupation? Perhaps for some, but most people know that there's so much more to life than one's job or occupation, especially when we take into account the social and economic challenges that we face in the 21st century.

As we move forward in the 21st century, we find that our own personal lives are subjected to political and economic forces that transcend the borders of our homeland. Our community and family life are disrupted and governed by forces that seem out of our control as we see a rise in single parent headed households, suicides, drug addiction, domestic violence, abuse, and bullying all over the United States. Sociologists remind us that in order to understand your personal troubles more fully, coming to grips with your sociological imagination is essential because it will enable you to see how your personal troubles and your higher education are connected to larger societal patterns.

Furthermore, developing your sociological understanding will allow you to gain greater insight into how the demands and pressures of our social institutions—e.g., economy and education—impact the quality of our lives. For example, there is a growing recognition among American citizens that our nation's workforce is becoming increasingly diverse as a result of socio-demographic factors, accelerated global migration, and civil rights legislation. In response, colleges and universities all over the nation have made more of an effort to help their students develop more of a well-rounded view of race relations, diversity, and international issues. One initiative widely practiced in American higher education is requiring undergraduate students to take diversity or multicultural courses in the hopes of helping students develop the knowledge, attitudes, and skills needed to make our nation more democratic and just (Banks, 1996; Downey & Torrecilha, 1994). According to the Association of American Colleges and Universities (AAC&U, 2013a), American higher education plays a significant role in helping students become sensitive to other cultures in a culturally diverse global community as well as preparing them to meet the challenges of responsible citizenship needed to work in an era of rapid societal and economic change.

In other words, entering into higher education is another defining moment in your life that provides you with the opportunity to rediscover who you are, what you are capable of, and what you can ultimately contribute to the world. While in college, your life is not entirely consumed with your job trying to pay off your debts to make ends meet—i.e., struggling to pay your basic living expenses such as food, clothing, shelter, and health care. You have the freedom now to choose not only your major or field of interest, but how you will develop the knowledge and those necessary capacities and skills to become a better person who can contribute to making our nation more democratic and just.

The AAC&U points out that one of the most urgent challenges that students, faculty, and administrators face in American higher education is:

> To ensure that all students develop both a rich understanding of the world they inherit—through studies in the humanities, arts, social sciences, and sciences—and the practical knowledge and capacities graduates need to help solve the difficult problems they will inevitably confront in the workplace, in their own lives, and as active

participants in a diverse and globally engaged democracy
(quoted in AAC& U's strategic plan, 2013a, p. 3).

So you see, when we apply our sociological imagination, we begin
to see that there is so much more value and purpose in acquiring
a higher education that goes well beyond just developing one's
knowledge and skills simply to earn a living in the job market.

Furthermore, thinking sociologically enables us to become
more mindful of the broader economic trends that impact individuals' employability. For example, the AAC&U's 2013 national
online survey of the business and nonprofit sectors revealed that
employers are more likely to hire college graduates who are better
prepared to work in a competitive global economy that is still coping with the lingering effects of the Great Recession (2007–2009)
(AAC&U, 2013b; Sternberg, 2013). If you are wondering about
what employers in the private and nonprofit economic sectors are
looking for or value the most in today's college graduates, then you
are applying your sociological imagination. Good for you!

More recently, the AAC&U (2018) conducted a national online
study of 501 executives and 500 hiring managers in both the
private and nonprofit economic sectors that revealed what these
employers are looking for in today's college graduates regardless
of their major. For example, the national online study revealed
that executives and hiring managers value most highly the following skills and capacities for social responsibility:

Skills

1. Oral communication (executives at 80% and hiring managers
   at 90%)

2. Written communication (executives at 76% and hiring managers at 78%)

3. Self-motivated, initiative, proactive: ideas/solutions (executives at 76% and hiring managers at 85%)

4. Critical thinking/analytical reasoning (executives at 78% and hiring managers at 84%)

5. Able to work independently: prioritize, manage time (executives at 77% and hiring managers at 85%)

Capacities for social responsibility

1. Ethical judgment and decision-making (executives at 77% and hiring managers at 87%)

2. Able to work effectively in teams (executives at 77% and hiring managers at 87%)

3. Can demonstrate continuous learning by applying knowledge/skills to real-world settings (executives at 76% and hiring managers at 87%)

(AAC&U, 2018)

In addition, AAC&U's 2013 national online study revealed that at least 9 in 10 out of 318 employers want their prospective hires to demonstrate capacities for social responsibility such as integrity and intercultural skills (AAC&U, 2013b).

Whether you have a major or are undeclared at this time, I encourage you to get involved with your university's career development center so that you can take advantage of its many resources to support your job search, skills and career or professional development. Educators point out that early involvement with career development services on college campuses can be very beneficial for students. For example, in a recent survey that was conducted of college graduates by Greenwood Hall, an education technology company, many college graduates had indicated that they felt unprepared entering into the workforce because they did not utilize any career development services while in college (Bidwell, 2015).

Furthermore, based on the AAC&U's research findings mentioned above, if you are concerned about your future prospects for employment, the first and most important step for you is to find out where you are at with your skills and capacities for social responsibility. The key here is to rediscover who you are and what you are capable of, especially in meeting the demands of responsible global citizenship. Thus, now is the time to engage in self exploration to identify your interests, skills, and capacities for social responsibility in order to match them up with your major, career, or professional objectives. Engaging in self exploration can help empower you to become more active in changing your life for the better. In addition, as you explore your skills and capacities for social responsibility, you can gain more insight into understanding yourself and others.

Exercise 1

Matching your interests, skills, and capacities for social responsibility with your major, career, or profession

✓ In a MS Word document using 12 pt. font, answer all of the questions below. Provide in-text citations to demonstrate that you are using *Sociology in Practice: Our Prescription for Living* as a source. You choose the Citation Style that you are most comfortable with using—e.g., MLA, APA, etc.

1. Identify at least three examples that demonstrate what it means for you to have a sociological understanding of the role of higher education (Hint: review pages 35–39).

2. How does thinking sociologically help you become more aware of your employability? Be sure to explain what the AAC&U's 2013 and 2018 national online surveys are as well as highlight their major findings by identifying all of the skills and capacities for social responsibility that are presented in these online studies.

3. Identify your major and career or professional interests. If you are undeclared, do the best you can to identify and explain what your career or professional interests may be.

4. What or who inspired you to choose your major; or if undeclared, why are you interested in the type of career or profession that you have identified above?

5. From the AAC&U's 2013 and 2018 national online surveys, identify three skills and three capacities for social responsibility that you think you will need in order to be successful in your major and career or profession. Be sure to explain why these particular skills and capacities for social responsibility are important. In addition, for each skill and capacity for social responsibility that you have chosen, identify and explain what your strengths and weaknesses are.

6. What types of college courses, workshops, seminars, programs or activities can help you further develop and strengthen your skills and capacities for social responsibility that you have identified in #5 above? Be sure to provide a rational to explain why each type would be beneficial to you.

PART TWO

DEVELOPING AND APPLYING YOUR SOCIOLOGICAL IMAGINATION IS A SOCIAL RESPONSIBILITY

Sociology's Beginning

In Part 2, we will explore and address the following topics:

- The emergence of sociology over 175 years ago and how sociology is more relevant today than it was since its beginning.
- Industrialization and the beginning of capitalism.
- Thinking sociologically is a social responsibility in the 21st century.
- The impact of income and wealth inequality in the 21st century.
- The impact of student loan debt and its challenges in the 21st century.

Over 175 years ago, the intellectual and humanist pioneers of sociology—Auguste Comte and Karl Marx—along with the rest of Western Europe were confronted with extraordinary social, economic, and political crises of epic proportions. The very basis of how people made a living was turned upside down as a consequence of the Industrial Revolution that began in England (circa 1780s–1849) (Giddens, 1987). The Industrial Revolution is marked by the advent of power-driven machinery for the purpose of mass producing goods and their distribution that forced many people to leave their close-knit farming communities to work as low-wage earners in factories in order to survive. This migration for survival not only created the rapid growth of urban life but also transformed Europe from an agrarian to an industrial economy.

As a young boy growing up in France, Auguste Comte (1798–1867) was engulfed in a state of social crisis. Social order in France was divided and in a state of decline (Seidman, 1994). On one end, Comte witnessed how the Catholic Church, monarchy and aristocracy ruled with absolute power and domination. For example, anyone who questioned or opposed the authoritarian rulers' power and knowledge in their quest for truth was beaten, imprisoned, or exiled. But, on the other end of the spectrum, there was a movement of moral and intellectual development that was created by the Enlightenment in the late 17th century (Seidman, 1994). Comte was deeply troubled and confused by the moral teachings of the Catholic church as he tried to reconcile the abusive behavior of the clerics while, at the same time, they were preaching about Jesus Christ's example of "turning the other cheek" when he was being persecuted.

Comte, like many others searching for a better way of life, embraced the moral and ethical vision of the Enlightenment to create a civil society—a society in which its governing authority respects and protects the well-being of all its citizens, encourages fairness and freedom of thought based on reason (Seidman, 1994). Unlike the clerical and aristocratic rulers who believed that the universe was governed by God's Will, Comte, like the astronomers and physicists of his time, believed that the universe could be uncovered by means of science and empirical research. Scientific reasoning was also on the rise with the creation of mechanized production which led to the Industrial Revolution—the beginning of modern capitalism (Giddens, 1987; Seidman, 1994). Even though the ruling elite of the church and aristocracy was challenged by the rising power of the industrialists, the masses suffered greatly. The industrialists profited enormously at the expense of their laborers working long hours for low wages as mentioned earlier. Deaths were not uncommon even among women and children working with unsafe machines and in dangerous working conditions.

Inspired by science and the moral and ethical vision of the Enlightenment, Comte strongly believed that science was humanity's only hope for a better way of life. He was perplexed by the fact that if there was a science that studied the stars (astronomy) and a science that studied the plants (botany), then why wasn't there a science that studied society? Thus, it became obvious for Comte to create a "science of society" known as sociology in order to cure his state of perplexity and embrace his longing for a better social world.

Karl Marx (1818–1883) was born in Germany and grew up in the midst of the Industrial Revolution. During Marx's lifetime, Germany was ruled by a very conservative landed nobility steeped in religious tradition that demanded submission to authority and tolerated very little social change and innovation (Seidman, 1994). As a result, Germany was slow to industrialize. But, the moral and ethical vision of the Enlightenment inspired many people, including Marx, in Germany, especially among the educated and political elite. Like Comte, Marx embraced science as having a critical role in liberating humanity from the capitalists' onslaught of oppression and exploitation against the working class (Seidman, 1994). However, unlike France, Germany lacked the social and political will to overthrow the landed aristocracy. Moreover, the German Enlighteners believed that social change should only come about by implementing new ideas rather than by a revolutionary movement (Seidman, 1994).

As Marx grew older, the more the peasants and laborers became discontented with their quality of life as their working conditions worsened along with an increase in unsanitary housing and disease. Even more frustrating for Marx, there was no viable movement to challenge the ruling class, including the government (Seidman, 1994). After graduating with a doctorate in philosophy from the University of Berlin, Marx wrote and spoke out in opposition of the German government and the ruling class's economic pursuits at the expense of the working class (Ritzer and Stepnisky, 2013). On one hand, Marx welcomed and appreciated the technological advancement that marked the beginning of modern capitalism—i.e., the creation of machines for mass production. But, on the other hand, as capitalism unfolded, Marx recognized that people cared very little about reaching one's full potential or expressing their creative capacities. For example, from Marx's perspective, the capitalists valued their profits earned from selling their products much more so than the labor of the working class—i.e., the actual work or labor that went into producing products was valued much less than the products sold (Ritzer and Stepnisky, 2013; Seidman, 1994).

The German government did not appreciate Marx's opposition against its political affairs and as such he was perceived as a political radical and could not secure an academic appointment anywhere in Germany. Ultimately, he was exiled to Paris, France where he continued to criticize the German government's lack of concern for improving the quality of life for the working class (Seidman, 1994). In Paris, he met his co-author, Friedrich Engels, the son of a wealthy industrialist, who acquainted Marx more fully with the real working conditions of the working class (Seidman,

1994). Marx was not only vocal about sharing his concerns and ideas about how the quality of life was in a state of decline for the working class, but he also joined workers' organizations in support of the movement to improve the working conditions and wages for the working class.

You may know of Marx as a communist revolutionary from your previous studies. But what you may not know or gave little thought to up until now, is the fact that Marx engaged in the first sociological study of the nature of capitalism and its effects on humans (Ritzer and Stepnisky, 2013; Seidman, 1994). Of particular interest to Marx was how humans actively express their true nature, and he considered human labor to be one of the primary active expressions of our true nature (Ritzer and Stepnisky, 2013; Seidman, 1994). Marx embraced Comte's vision of a "science of society" to characterize the development of modern society as a consequence of human productivity in the form of economic labor or paid labor (Seidman, 1994).

Central to Marx's theory of human productivity as paid labor is the idea that capitalism creates the following class divisions: the capitalist class (bourgeoisie) who own the means of production—i.e., factories, tools, raw materials, and machines; and the working class (proletariat) who sell their labor in order to gain access to the means of production so that they can make a living (Ritzer and Stepnisky, 2013; Seidman, 1994). Furthermore, as mentioned earlier, Marx points out that because the main focus of the capitalist class is to make profit rather than to ensure that the working class reaches their full human potential—i.e., intellectual capacity and creative abilities—a class conflict or struggle emerges. According to Marx, it's the working class who suffers the most in this class conflict because the workers' labor is valued the least and as a consequence the workers become alienated from their true sense of self (Ritzer and Stepnisky, 2013). In other words, the workers lose a sense of purpose or fulfillment in their lives; and as a result, they are unable to grasp the potential they have as human beings.

However, Marx believed that as science reveals the true nature behind the class struggle, the working class can achieve what he refers to as a class consciousness (Ritzer and Stepnisky, 2013; Seidman, 1994). By class consciousness, Marx meant that the workers would become aware of how the capitalist class has exploited them and kept them from reaching their full human potential (Ritzer and Stepnisky, 2013). And lastly, in Marx's view, when the working class achieves class consciousness they must take action to ultimately overthrow the capitalist class from power through a revolution to prepare the way for a communist society (Ritzer and Stepnisky, 2013). As mentioned earlier, Marx is well known for his radical communist ideas that are clearly not scientific nor did they become a reality. Furthermore, Marx did very little theorizing about communism and its impact on humans (Ritzer and Stepnisky, 2013). But nevertheless, Marx's scientific inquiry into the growth and expansion of capitalism, especially its effects on human potential, contributed immensely to the beginning of sociology over 175 years ago.

Connecting the Past to the Present and Future

Moreover, Comte's vision for sociology, also known as the "science of society," to address the moral, political, and economic crises confronting the beginning of modern society inspired Marx to address the downfalls of capitalism which we find to be more relevant today than ever before (Ritzer and Stepnisky, 2013). Indeed, as early as 2012, in the wake of the Great Recession, research studies revealed that more than half of recent college graduates are either not employed, looking for a job, or underemployed—i.e., in jobs that do not require a college degree (Newman, 2014). And the number of college graduates who have been out of work for more than six months has more than tripled from 13% in 2000 to roughly 44% in 2012 (Newman, 2014). However, although the economy has shown some signs of improvement with a decreasing unemployment rate in recent years, in 2015, roughly 45 percent of college graduates were working in jobs that did not require a college degree (Economic Policy Institute, 2016). Furthermore, the Class of 2016 experienced job quality deterioration along with lack of wage growth or stagnate wages (Economic Policy Institute, 2016).

To be clear, this downward economic trend that is impacting the employability of college graduates is not solely a college graduate phenomenon. Nor can *individual explanations*—i.e., individual deficiencies or personal flaws—adequately explain this dramatic decline in the job prospects for college graduates (Machum & Clow, 2015; Newman, 2014). If we were to focus exclusively on the personal flaws or deficiencies of college graduates, then we would overlook the broader societal forces that may have impacted their job prospects (Carnevale, Hanson, & Gulish, 2013). Therefore, in order for us to capture these broader societal forces, we need to apply our sociological imagination by taking into account its first lesson. The first lesson in applying the sociological imagination is this:

> The individual can understand his own experience and gauge his own fate only by locating himself within his period, that he can know his own chances in life only by becoming aware of those of all individuals in his circumstances (Mills, 1959, p. 5).

Indeed, thinking sociologically, enables us to see that everyone in the workforce, young or old, including those with a bachelor's degree, a two-year associate's degree, or a high school diploma were impacted by broader economic trends such as corporate cost-saving measures that began in the 1970s and were more intense during the Great Recession in 2007–2009 (Samuel, 2012). If you will recall, at the heart of Marx's critique of the expansion of capitalism is its inability to facilitate the growth of human potential of the working class because the central purpose of the capitalists is profit maximization. In fact, in order to maximize profit in the wake of the Great Recession, capitalist employers employed the following cost-saving measures: laid off workers, hired fewer people, including college graduates, and reduced their financial contributions to worker 401(k) retirement plans (Dobratz, Waldner, and Buzzell, 2012). The bottom-line here is for employers to maximize their profit by getting their employees to work harder for less pay, including picking up the slack of their co-workers who were either laid off or lost their jobs entirely.

The post-World War II manufacturing economy that built our middle class in the 1950s when the economy was fueled by consumers spending their rising wages received from work is no longer a reality. Unfortunately, in the last 45 years, significant economic growth has occurred for the top 20 percent—corporate executives and politicians—who make at least $200,000 annually; but the reverse is true for the majority of the workforce. For example, since 1970–2014, the percentage of all income going to those in working class and middle class households at $25,000–$74,000 annually who make up 80 percent has declined, whereas the percentage of all income going to the top 20 percent increased (Pew Research Center, 2015b; see Figure 2.1).

FIGURE 2.1

The share of aggregate income held by middle-income households plunged from 1970 to 2014 and is now less than the share held by upper-income households

% of U.S. aggregate household income held by lower-, middle- and upper-income households

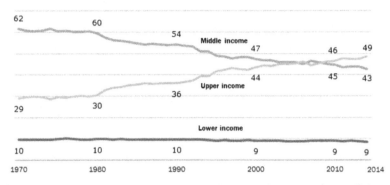

Note: Households are assigned to income tiers based on their size-adjusted income in the calendar year prior to the survey year. Their unadjusted incomes are then totaled to compute the share of an income tier in the U.S. aggregate household income. Shares may not add to 100% due to rounding

Source: Pew Research Center analysis of the Current Population Survey, Annual Social and Economic Supplements, 1971 to 2015

PEW RESEARCH CENTER

SOURCE: Pew Research Center, "The American Middle Class is Losing Ground" http://www.pewsocialtrends.org/2015/12/09/4-middle-class-incomes-fall-further-behind-upper-tier-incomes/.

The income gap between the rich and the working class is the widest it has ever been in U.S. history, as we saw millions of people loosing not only their jobs, but also their homes, and pension funds during the Great Recession (Etzioni, 2014; Leicht and Fitzgerald, 2007). However, measuring wealth is a much better indicator of a family's economic worth and power because it consists of the value of all the family's assets minus debts (Pew Research Center, 2015b; Sernau, 2017). Wealth includes the value of corporate stocks and other financial investments, homeownership, automobiles, businesses, and savings (Sernau, 2017). And interestingly, the wealth gap between the upper-income and middle-income Americans is much wider than the income gap and had reached a record high in 2013. For example, in 2013, the wealth for upper-income families ($650,074) was nearly 7 times as much as the wealth of middle-income families ($98,057) (Pew Research Center, 2015b). But even more startling, from 1983–2013, the middle-income families' wealth only increased by 2%; whereas the wealth for upper-income families had doubled from 323,402 in 1983 to 650,074 (see Figure 2.2). In addition, the wealth gap is even wider along racial lines. For example, the White household median wealth rose from being 10 times higher than the Black household median wealth in 2010 to being 13 times higher in 2013 even as economic recovery measures were being implemented (Pew Research Center, 2014).

FIGURE 2.2

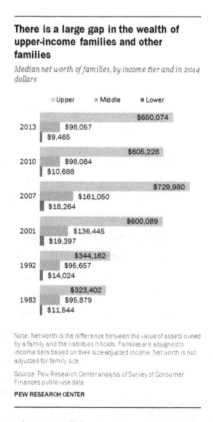

There is a large gap in the wealth of upper-income families and other families

Median net worth of families, by income tier and in 2014 dollars

Upper   Middle   Lower

2013
$650,074
$98,057
$9,465

2010
$605,228
$98,084
$10,688

2007
$729,980
$161,050
$18,264

2001
$600,089
$136,445
$19,397

1992
$344,162
$95,657
$14,024

1983
$323,402
$95,879
$11,544

Note: Net worth is the difference between the value of assets owned by a family and the liabilities it holds. Families are assigned to income tiers based on their size-adjusted income. Net worth is not adjusted for family size.

Source: Pew Research Center analysis of Survey of Consumer Finances public-use data

PEW RESEARCH CENTER

SOURCE: Pew Research Center, "The American Middle Class is Losing Ground"

Moreover, from 2000–2010, the majority of families filing for bankruptcy were of the middle class (Dobratz et al., 2012; Leicht and Fitzgerald, 2007). What is responsible for the rise in the middle-class bankruptcy phenomenon? Sociologists point out that the high cost of living, job and income losses, divorce, as well as health care expenses have all contributed to an overwhelming number of middle-class families filing bankruptcy claims annually (Dobratz et al., 2012; Leicht and Fitzgerald, 2007). A key marker for increasing one's wealth is home ownership which is one of the basic necessities of achieving the American Dream. And unfortunately, home ownership rates for racial and ethnic minorities—e.g., Blacks and Hispanics—is below 50 percent at 42.3 percent and 45.5 percent respectively, compared to Whites at 72.2 percent (United States Census Bureau, 2017). In addition, many more Americans are faced with more employers or corporations employing cost-saving measures such as low-paying jobs that offer very little financial security and no benefits, making it more difficult for people, especially college graduates to buy or own their home (Etzioni, 2014; Samuel, 2012).

In addition, commercial banks and other financial organizations engage in investment banking as well as other financial services to accumulate capital by making it easier for consumers to borrow money (Derber, 2011; Etzioni, 2014). As a result of banks providing easy access to credit coupled with the increase in low-paying jobs and income loss or stagnation, the economy is now fueled by consumers borrowing money from commercial banks and other financial lenders to pay off their purchases and investments, including education due to the rising costs of higher education. For example, Sallie Mae, one of the leading private student loan lenders, has contributed to the problem of student loan debt of over 1.5 trillion dollars now being the second-largest source of debt, after home mortgages for consumers in the United States (Derber, 2011; Dynarski, 2015).

As we use our sociological imagination to take into account these broader economic trends addressed above, we see that as the working class and middle class households fall further into debt, more and more college graduates are struggling to find decent jobs that not only pay their basic living expenses, including car loans, but also utilize the full value of their college education (Davidson, 2014). And because many more recent college graduates already are in debt when they enter the workforce, they find themselves having to work unsatisfying and unfulfilling jobs that do not advance their human potential just so that they can make ends meet, including paying down their student loans (Davidson, 2014; Newman, 2014).

Reality check!

Like any loan, student loans accrue interest. By the time most students pay off a $30,100 (national average for bachelor's degree recipients only in 2015) loan, they will pay over $8,299 in interest at a fixed rate of 5.05 percent (fixed rate for Stafford Loans in 2018–19). That's a total of $38,399 to pay off a student loan. The average earner will need at least 9 years to pay this in full.

—Source: New York Times at https://www.nytimes.com/interactive/2016/your-money/student-loan-repayment-calculator.html?_r=0

Recent data reveal that the average student loan debt is at $28,950 and is expected to increase significantly due to rising tuition costs and income stagnation (Economic Policy Institute, 2016; The Project on Student Debt, 2015). Consequently, just like their parents, but even more so, these recent college graduates of the Millennial Generation (born between 1980 and late 1990s) find themselves so in debt to those whom they owe money—i.e., banks and other financial lenders have control over their lives. Indeed, in his eye opening account of *Who Rules America? The Triumph of the Corporate Rich*, sociologist William Domhoff (2014) points out that in 2011, the majority of Americans at 67 percent believed that "Corporations, banks, and other financial institutions have too much power in the United States" (p. x). These economic forces have impacted the Millennial Generation in such a way that we see 36 percent, a significant number of young adults between the ages of 18 to 31, moving back home to live with their parents (Davidson, 2014, Pew Research Center, 2013). And the majority of them at roughly 60 percent also receive financial support from their parents (Davidson, 2014). Experts refer to this new emerging trend within the Millennial Generation as "the boomerang kids" (Davidson, 2014; Ludwig, 2013).

Did you know...

... That almost 40 percent (39 percent) of college students said "they felt so depressed that it was difficult to function."
—American College Health Association
Fall 2016 report

Is it a sign of failure for college graduates who "boomerang" back home to live with their parents because they are unable to financially support themselves? Your response would depend, of course, on how well you apply your sociological imagination. For example, if you are focusing only on individual explanations in your explanation of the boomerang phenomenon, then you would point out how incompetent or financially illiterate these college graduates are in planning their long-term financial goals beyond graduation. Or perhaps another individual explanation could be about how you think these college graduates feel a sense of entitlement because they think they deserve a decent job for merely graduating from college. But notice how these individual explanations tend to blame these boomerang kids for not measuring up to certain cultural or societal standards—e.g., American individualism and meritocracy. In other words, it is their own fault for not living up to their potential because in America, you only need to work hard to achieve success. And furthermore, when only focusing on individual explanations there is a tendency to stereotype or overgeneralize who these boomerang kids are and what they think by implying that "they all must be like that"—i.e., incompetent, lazy, or have unrealistic expectations of themselves.

However, when you begin to apply your sociological imagination, your focus is not only on individual explanations, including yourself, but also broader social, cultural, and economic forces. For example, as you think about financing the cost of your higher education, keep in mind that for over 60 percent of college students this means taking on student loan debt. For the first part in Exercise 2, use the following link to access "The Student Loan Calculator" to address the broader economic picture of taking on loans and repaying them after graduation. After you complete the first part, go to the second part to click on the link to find out where you are at in the distribution of Americans by income. And lastly, in the third part, click on the link to address where you think America should be in terms of its income distribution versus America's actual income distribution; and then, enter in your gender, race/ethnicity, educational attainment, age, etc. to address how the broader social and economic forces impact your socioeconomic status.

Exercise 2

1. https://www.nytimes.com/interactive/2017/your-money/
   student-loan-repayment-calculator.html

2. http://www.pewresearch.org/fact-tank/2018/09/06/
   are-you-in-the-american-middle-class/

3. http://inequality.is/real

The Millennials have higher levels of unemployment and poverty as well as lower levels of income and wealth (Pew Research Center, 2014a). And to rub salt in the wound, Millennials are also more alienated from social institutions such as politics and law, religion, and family than its two predecessors—Baby Boomers and Generation X. For example, a recent Pew Research survey found that half of the Millennials (50 percent) are now moving away from the traditional political parties of Republican or Democrat and identifying themselves as politically independent; whereas 39 percent of Generation X (ages 34–49) and 37 percent of Baby Boomers (ages 50–68) feel politically independent (Pew Research Center, 2014b). In addition, more and more Millennials are moving away from organized religion as almost 30 percent (29%) have not claimed any religious affiliation compared with 21 percent of Generation X and only 16 percent of Baby Boomers not claiming any religious affiliation (Pew Research Center, 2014b).

Lastly, the Millennials, more so than Generation X and the Baby Boomers, are experiencing a lack of empathy, distrust, and disconnect not only from politicians but also other people in general (Pew Research Center, 2014b) (see Figure 2.3). Only 19 percent of the Millennials had indicated that, "Generally speaking, most people can be trusted" in a 2012 General Social Survey (GSS) (Pew Research Center, 2014b). And not only are half of the Millennials feeling disconnected from both Republican and Democratic parties, but just 31 percent had indicated that there is a major "difference in what the Republican and Democratic parties stand for" (Pew Research Center, 2014b).

FIGURE 2.3

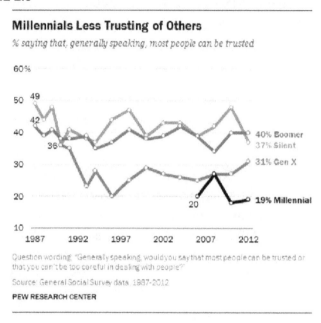

Millennials Less Trusting of Others

% saying that, generally speaking, most people can be trusted

Question wording: "Generally speaking, would you say that most people can be trusted or that you can't be too careful in dealing with people?"

Source: General Social Survey data 1987-2012

PEW RESEARCH CENTER

SOURCE: Pew Research Center, "Millennials Less Trusting of Others," http://www.pewsocialtrends. org/2014/03/07/millennials-in-adulthood/.

In a more recent Pew Research survey that was conducted in 2014, it was also pointed out that Millennials are distancing themselves from the social institution of family and marriage (Pew Research Center, 2014b). For example, in 2013, only 26 percent of the Millennials (ages 18–31) were married; while at the same life stage in 1980, 48 percent of the Baby Boomers were married, and 36 percent of Generation X were married in 1997 (Pew Research

Center, 2014b). One of the most common explanations that Millennials give for putting off marriage is that they do not feel financially secure or have yet to achieve financial independence.

Like Marx, Émile Durkheim (1858–1917) was also inspired by Comte's vision of sociology to address the social, economic, and political crises that had emerged in Europe as a result of industrialization over 135 years ago. Durkheim was born in France and grew up in the beginning of the modern age. In his earlier years of schooling he was very disappointed by the lack of scientific and moral attention given to address the social and economic breakdown of communities (Ritzer and Stepnisky, 2013; Seidman, 1994). When Durkheim entered university for the first time circa 1870s, he wanted to study a discipline that directly addressed the issues of moral and practical guidance for society. But he noted that there was no suitable discipline that took up this humanitarian task. And since sociology was not a discipline back then, he unhappily settled for studying psychology and philosophy of science. However, Durkhiem was inspired by Comte's vision of sociology so much so that it drove him to be very active in establishing sociology as a discipline in higher education as well as laying its scientific foundation. Sometime after graduating from École Normale Supérieure, a very selective and prestigious French university in 1882, he created the first two courses of sociology that were taught in a university.

Durkheim was particularly interested in scientifically examining how societies struggle to maintain unity, cohesion, and stability. He was centrally concerned about the effects of industrialization— i.e., societies shifting from a simple, close-knit farming community to an emerging modern society that is characterized by complex divisions of labor resulting in an increase of individualism where people perform specialized tasks in order to survive. From his research, he noted that as societies begin to industrialize to become modern, the moral cohesion and stability of those societies weaken (Ritzer and Stepnisky, 2013; Seidman, 1994). Consequently, people are not as close to one another and are insufficiently integrated into communities, families, schools, or even churches (Derber, 2011; Ritzer and Stepnisky, 2013). There is no sense of a strong unified community creating a fulfilling and meaningful life. Much emphasis is placed on how our own individual selves need to succeed in life. In other words, developing a moral compass relies more on self-interest than on the community's well-being (Derber, 2011).

According to Durkheim, when people are closely knit and well integrated into their communities and social institutions, they experience a rush of emotional intensity that is uplifting, drawing them closer to one another. Unfortunately, in a recent study that was conducted by the Cooperative Institute Program (CIRP) at UCLA's Higher Education Research Institute, it was found that there was a significant increase of first-year college students entering college depressed (CIRP, 2014). As a result, psychiatrists have identified the declining emotional health of college freshman as a public health issue (Schwarz, 2015). More and more students are pointing out that they feel overwhelmed due to the pressures of competing in a global economy as well as feeling higher levels of stress as a result of focusing more on academics and socializing less (Schwarz, 2015).

PART THREE

YOUR SOCIOLOGICAL IMAGINATION IN PRACTICE

Setting the Stage

In Part 3, we will explore and address the following topics:

- The major sources of stress in America in the 21st century.
- The impact of rapid social change.
- Losing hope in the American Dream.
- Applying your sociological imagination to your personal trouble.
- Defining the role of civil society and social responsibility.

A s we move forward in the 21st century, Americans are on edge concerning where America is headed in the future. This past 2016 presidential election of Donald J. Trump has generated intense feelings of uncertainty and anxiety about their future outlook, especially among Millennials, as there seems to be no meaningful solutions presented to resolve America's big social and economic issues ranging from racial tensions, income and wealth inequality to terrorism and mass shootings

(American Psychological Association, 2017). Moreover, family life has changed quite considerably over the past 50 years—for example, divorce and family disruption is higher, single parenting is rising, people are waiting longer to get married, both parents spend more time at work, and consequently, schools are addressing many problems families deal with at home such as training in moral values dealing with drug and alcohol addiction, suicide, body shaming, sexuality, violence, and bullying.

A 2017 American Psychological Association (APA) research study on stress in America reported that Americans' stress levels have significantly increased for the first time in 10 years. One of the contributing factors to this increase in stress has to do with Americans' future outlook. This new APA study revealed that 66 percent of Americans feel stressed about the future of America (APA, 2017). In addition, almost 6 out of 10 Millennials (58 percent) consider the 2016 election outcome "as a very or somewhat significant source of stress" compared to 45 percent of Baby Boomers and only 39 percent of Generation X feeling stressed about the 2016 election outcome (APA, 2017).

Moreover, the majority of Americans feel stressed about money, work, and the economy; however, Americans cited the following contributing factors that were responsible for adding to their stress in the last 10 years: economy (44 percent), terrorism (34 percent), and mass shootings/gun violence (31 percent) (APA, 2017). In addition, the increase in media coverage of police violence and shootings that led to the deaths of many Black Americans in recent years, has also contributed to a significant rise in Americans feeling more stressed, especially among Black Americans. For example, within just a five-month period (August 2016 to January 2017), the 2017 APA survey found that the percentage of Americans who are feeling stressed about police violence toward minorities increased from 36 percent to 44 percent. However, within this same five-month period, Black Americans are more likely to report feeling stressed about police violence toward minorities—for example, the percentage of Black Americans who are feeling stressed rose from 68 percent to 71 percent (APA, 2017).

The Millennials, like many Americans, are barely hanging on to the American Dream, hoping to live a much "richer and fuller life" in the land of the free. However, the Millennials, as the first generation to come of age in the 21st century, are beginning to realize that the American Dream's promise of equal opportunity for all and personal fulfillment is becoming hollow. For example, a recent study of 18-to 29-year olds conducted by Harvard's Institute of Politics (2015), found that about half of the Millennials believed that the American Dream was dead (e.g., 48 percent believed the American Dream was dead versus 49 percent considered the American Dream alive). And while half of the Millennials still support the American Dream's promise of working hard to earn financial independence to become more responsible citizens, many Millennials know that it is not enough to base their success and personal fulfillment in life solely on the economic conception of the American Dream. We must also take into account how the rapid societal changes like sudden economic crises, natural disasters, family disruptions, mass shootings, wars, and terrorism have brought about not only increased levels of stress and anxiety, but also feelings of intense uncertainty as a result of things changing so quickly. Things have changed so quickly over the last 40 to 50 years that old cultural standards, norms, or customs no longer work in terms of bringing about formidable solutions, especially when Millennials point out the inability of political parties, family and community life to generate social engagement, commitment, and trust (Hauhart, 2015).

And even though we are well informed everyday by the news reports of these life-changing societal events and trends, there is an overwhelming sense that we are losing control over what's happening, nor are we able to meaningfully explain why it's happening, let alone take meaningful steps to resolve it. Furthermore, because our cultural individualistic ethos stresses how we as individuals need to succeed in fulfilling our self-interests, we tend to overlook the morality and well-being of our communities (Ritzer and Stepnisky, 2013; Derber, 2011). As a consequence, we have a strong tendency to view our struggles or hardships as a private matter that can be resolved only by addressing our own private state of affairs involving immediate relations with other people.

To date, the U.S. government and the corporate community have yet to take meaningful steps to address the widening income and wealth gaps between the rich and the working class (Economic Policy Institute, 2016). During the Obama administration, the recovery measures of the Great Recession primarily bailed out Wall Street, and intensified the implementation of cost-saving measures by corporations (Domhoff, 2014; Dobratz, et al. 2012). And now, at the time of this writing, almost ten years into the recovery, Trump's administration is stimulating and protecting economic growth at the very top by strengthening investment banking and corporate cost-saving measures, thereby maximizing the financial rewards of corporate executives through capital market investments rather than investing in workforce development and wage growth. Consequently, the economic foundation of the American working and middle class families is further weakened. Unfortunately, when power inequalities exist in democratic political and economic systems like ours, sociologists tell us that a growing distrust of the government among its citizens can happen; and consequently, its citizens feel left to their own devices, especially in looking out for their own well-being (Cook, 2015). Indeed, public trust in the federal government was at its highest point in 1964 at 77 percent, but declined sharply through the 1970s; and now, only 18% of Americans say they "trust the government in Washington always or most of the time" (Pew Research Center, 2017; see Figure 3.1).

Is there any wonder why Americans are feeling more stressed than ever in the last 10 years about the future outlook of America? And what about the growing alienation crisis of the Millennials?

FIGURE 3.1

Trust in the federal government remains near historic low

% who say they trust the federal government to do what is right just about always/most of the time ...

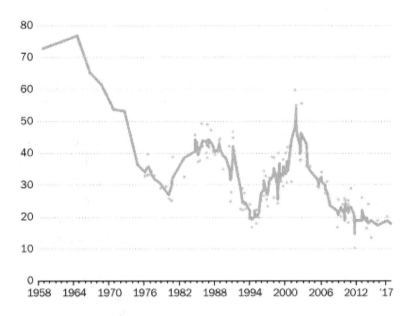

Notes: From 1976-2017 the trend line represents a three-survey moving average.
Source: Survey of U.S. adults conducted Nov. 29-Dec. 4, 2017.
Trend sources: Pew Research Center, National Election Studies, Gallup, ABC/Washington Post, CBS/New York Times, and CNN polls.

PEW RESEARCH CENTER

SOURCE: Pew Research Center, "Government Gets Lower Ratings for Handling Health Care, Environment, Disaster Response."

How can the American Dream, a profound cultural vision shared by many across racial, ethnic, economic, and political lines, guide us to a better way of life, especially as we work to resolve our own personal as well as societal problems? In order to address these important questions, we must employ the sociological framework that I proposed earlier in Part 1—that is, to engage you to apply your sociological imagination by critically examining how your personal troubles—e.g., depression, anxiety, alienation, suicide, drug addiction, divorce or family disruption, domestic violence, eating disorders, sexist and racist ideologies, etc.—also arise due to cultural and institutional forces. In doing so, we will gain deeper sociological insights into how our self is interconnected to the world we live in. In addition, we will be guided to see that our personal troubles cannot be solved solely by ourselves, but also involves transforming the culture, social institutions, and organizations that impact us as well. Furthermore, as we revisit the meaning of the American Dream, I want you to recall the meaning of civil society defined in Part 2 as—a society in which its governing authority respects and protects the well-being of all its citizens, encourages fairness and freedom of thought based on reason (Seidman, 1994). As we develop, strengthen, and apply our sociological understanding, we will gain more insight into our personal lives, including our personal troubles.

If we are to think seriously about transforming our culture, social institutions, and organizations for the better, then we must embrace this moral and ethical vision of developing a civil society. This moral and ethical vision of encouraging and protecting the well-being of everyone is nothing new; this profound vision of developing a civil society is what fueled the Enlightenment in the 17th century and is what eventually led to the Declaration of Independence of the United States of America. Sociologists remind us that our lives consist of "joint action, or what people do together" (Sandstrom, Martin, and Fine, 2010, p. 14). In addition, the meaning of joint action also recognizes that we are not only individuals, but we also belong to or are representatives of certain groups whether it be family, political, racial or ethnic. The fact that we have identities based on the groups we belong to or represent has important moral and ethical implications. In other words, everything that we do together has consequences for others whether it be good or bad (Sandstrom et al., 2010). And as we take into account the first question in our sociological framework—*how are activities patterned in our society?*—we see how our economy and education social institutions function to encourage you to develop and strengthen not only your academic and workplace skills, but also capacities of social responsibility such as ethical judgement and integrity, intercultural skills and continuous learning. All of these capacities of social responsibility are necessary ingredients for developing a civil society. There has always been an emphasis in higher education to develop your critical thinking, complex problem solving, and communication skills; but now, more than ever, the faculty in higher education are charged with helping you develop and strengthen your capacities of social responsibility to improve human relations which are the basis of a civil society.

However, if you are tempted to fall deeper into your personal troubles, you must counteract this temptation or feeling by using your sociological imagination to focus on the meaningful aspects of your lives, as well as address the root causes of your stress and anxiety. By applying your sociological imagination, you will be able to identify how your social psychological circumstances of what you are dealing with in your everyday life are connected as well as influenced by "the public issues of social structure"—i.e., the historical, institutional, and cultural forces. In so doing, you will take a more active role in your learning. Learning is meaningless unless it is connected to the way you think, act, and feel based on your lived experiences. Challenge yourselves to address the second question in our sociological framework—*where is society located in its history?*—by critically examining the progress we have made since World War II with respect to dealing with your personal trouble. Pay particular close attention to how social institutions (e.g., economy, politics and law, mass media, etc.) as well as culture have functioned to improve the quality of your life as well. As you do this, you will begin to see your quality of life and lived experiences in a much larger cultural and institutional context.

And lastly, tackle the third question in our sociological framework—*what kinds of people are produced in society?* From the previous question concerning whether or not progress has been made since WWII, you should begin to see the unique social and economic challenges that your generation faces now versus the Baby Boomer's social and economic circumstances at least 50 years ago. And as you address your future in terms of quality of life, professional and career prospects, think about how culture and social institutions—e.g., family, education, economy, health care, politics and law etc.—are providing you with opportunities to reach your fullest potential in preparing you to meet the demands of responsible global citizenship.

Thinking sociologically is taking social responsibility not only for ourselves but also society and the world because having this kind of awareness of ourselves helps us better understand why we are the we are or do the things we do and with that, we can begin to make our society better.

Exercise 3

Applied learning sociological imagination paper

✓ Apply the concept of the sociological imagination to your life to explain how **ONE** of your personal troubles could be a societal issue. In an MS Word document using 12 pt. font, address all five parts below. Provide in-text citations to demonstrate that you are using our course material as well as other relevant sources. You choose the Citation Style that you are most comfortable with using—e.g., MLA, APA, etc.

1. Introduce your own personal trouble and explain why you chose it. Then define and provide a detailed explanation of the concept of the sociological imagination. Provide examples using our course material as primary sources—e.g., assigned reading and lecture notes—to support your definition and explanation.

2. Explain why you think the sociological imagination can apply to your personal trouble. Be sure to make references to the course material by providing in-text citations to support your argument.

3. Demonstrate how your personal trouble can also be a societal or public issue. Focus on how culture, social institutions, and organizations impact your personal trouble. Be sure to define and explain how culture, each social institution and organization functions, as well as critically examine the progress we have made since World War II with respect to dealing with your personal trouble. In addition, you may use other source

material that can provide additional information—e.g., statistics, news article info etc.—about your personal trouble.

4. Identify the four benefits of having and applying your sociological understanding to your personal trouble. Be sure to apply all four benefits by explaining in great detail how each benefit has helped you address and deal with your personal trouble. You can find all four benefits of having a sociological understanding in our Week 1's Lecture Outline.

5. Don't forget your Works cited page! And, make sure that all of your in-text citations and Works cited page follow the format and style of your Citation Style.

REFERENCES

Abrams, A. (2014). How student loan debt hurts your health. *Time*. http://time.com/2854384/student-loan-debt-health/. Accessed July 10, 2016.

Adams, J. T. (1931). *The epic of America*. Boston, MA: Little, Brown, and Co.

Association of American Colleges and Universities. (2018). *Fulfilling the American Dream: Liberal Education and the Future of Work*. https://www.aacu.org/sites/default/files/files/LEAP/2018EmployerResearchReport.pdf. Accessed October 15, 2018.

Association of American Colleges and Universities. (2013a). Strategic plan 2013–2017: Big questions, urgent challenges: Liberal education and Americans' global future. https://www.aacu.org/about/strategicplan. Accessed December 8, 2014.

Association of American Colleges and Universities. (2013b). It takes more than a major: Employer priorities for college learning and student success. http://aacu.org/sites/default/files/files/LEAP/2013_EmployerSurvey.pdf. Accessed December 20, 2014.

American Psychological Association. (2017). Stress in America: Coping with change. http://www.apa.org/news/press/releases/

stress/2016/coping-with-change.PDF. Accessed September 22, 2017.

Banks, J. (1996). Multicultural literacy and curriculum reform. In C. Turner, M. Garcia, A. Nora, & L. I. Rendon (Eds.), *Racial and ethnic diversity in higher education*. ASHE Reader Series. Neeham Heights, MA: Simon and Schuster.

Bidwell, A. (2015). College grads question the return on investment of today's degrees. *U.S. News & World Report*. http://www.usnews.com/news/articles/2015/02/10/college-grads-question-the-return-on-investment-of-todays-degrees. Accessed April 15, 2015.

Buechler, S. (2014). Critical sociology. Paradigm Publishers.

Cain Miller, C. (2014, June 20). A college major matters even more in a recession. *The New York Times*.

Career Development Center. (2014). Major & career exploration. East Stroudsburg University. http://www4.esu.edu/students/career_services/career_exploration.cfm. Accessed December 23, 2014.

Carnevale, A., Hanson, A., & Gulish, A. (2013). *Failure to launch: Structural shift and the new lost generation*. Georgetown University. https://cew.georgetown.edu/cew-reports/failure-to-launch/. Accessed March, 2016.

Centers for Disease Control and Prevention. (2012). Higher education and income levels keys to better health, according to annual report on nation's health. http://www.cdc.gov/media/releases/2012/p0516_higher_education.html. Accessed March 7, 2015.

Cook, K. (2015). Institutions, trust, and social order. In E. Lawler, S. Thye, & J. Yoon (Eds.), *Order on the edge of chaos: Social psychology and the problem of social order*. New York, NY: Cambridge University Press.

Cooperative Institute Research Program. (2014). The American freshman: National norms fall 2014. http://www.heri.ucla.edu/

monographs/TheAmericanFreshman2014.pdf. Accessed June, 2015.

Davidson, A. (2014). It's official: The boomerang kids won't leave. *The New York Times Magazine*. http://www.nytimes .com/2014/06/22/magazine/its-official-the-boomerang-kids-wont-leave.html?_r=0#. Accessed June 25, 2014.

Derber, C. (2011). *The wilding of America*. 5th ed. New York, NY: Worth Publishers.

Dobratz, B., Waldner, L., & Buzzell, T. (2012). *Power, politics, and society: An introduction to political sociology*. Boston, MA: Allyn & Bacon.

Domhoff, G. (2014). *Who rules America? The triumph of the corporate rich*. Boston, MA: McGraw-Hill.

Downey, D., & Torrecilha, R. (1994). Sociology of race and ethnicity: Strategies for comparative multicultural courses. *Teaching Sociology, 22*, 237–247.

Dynarski, S. (2015). We're frighteningly in the dark about student debt. *The New York Times*. http://nyti.ms/1H9VdQk. Accessed March 21, 2015.

Economic Policy Institute. (2016). *The class of 2016: The labor market is still far from ideal for young graduates*. http://www .epi.org/publication/class-of-2016/. Accessed June 1, 2017.

Etzioni, A. (2014). Politics and culture in an age of austerity. *International Journal of Politics, Culture, and Society, 27*, 389–407.

Giddens, A. (1987). *Sociology: A brief but critical introduction*. (2nd ed.). New York, NY: Harcourt Brace Jovanovich, Publishers.

Harvard University Institute of Politics. (2015). Executive summary: Survey of young Americans' attitudes toward politics and public service. http://iop.harvard.edu/sites/default/files_new/pictures/151208_Harvard%20IOP%20Fall%202015%20Report.pdf. Accessed July 25, 2017.

Hauhart, R. (2015). American sociology's investigations of the American dream: Retrospect and prospect. *The American Sociologist*, 46(1), 65–98.

Leicht, K., & Fitzgerald, S. (2007). *Postindustrial peasants: The illusion of middle-class prosperity*. New York, NY: Worth Publishers.

Ludwig, R. (2013). How long is too long for boomerang kids to live with their parents? *The Huffington Post*. http://www.huffingtonpost.com/robi-ludwig/how-long-is-too-long_b_3748365.html. Accessed June 5, 2015.

Machum, S. & Clow, M. (2015). Commit sociology: Learn to be a critical thinker. *Humanity & Society*, 39(2), 189–212.

McGrath Goodman, L. (2015). Millennial College Graduates: Young, Educated, Jobless. *Newsweek*. http://www.newsweek.com/2015/06/05/millennial-college-graduates-young-educated-jobless-335821.html. Accessed June 5, 2015.

Mills, C. (1959). *The sociological imagination*. New York: NY: Oxford University Press.

Newman, D. (2015). *Sociology: Exploring the architecture of everyday life Brief Edition* (4th ed.). Los Angeles, CA: Sage Publications.

Pew Research Center. (2015a). *10 Facts about American workers*. http://www.pewresearch.org/fact-tank/2016/09/01/8-facts-about-american-workers/. Accessed August 15, 2016.

Pew Research Center. (2015b). *The American middle class is losing ground*. http://www.pewsocialtrends.org/2015/12/09/4-middle-class-incomes-fall-further-behind-upper-tier-incomes/. Accessed June 15, 2017.

Pew Research Center (2014). *Wealth inequality has widened along racial, ethnic lines since end of great recession*. http://www.pewresearch.org/fact-tank/2014/12/12/racial-wealth-gaps-great-recession/. Accessed October 7, 2017.

Pew Research Center. (2014a). *The rising cost of not going to college.* http://www.pewsocialtrends.org/files/2014/02/SDT-higher-ed-FINAL-02-11-2014.pdf. Accessed November 13, 2014.

Pew Research Center. (2014b). *Millennials in adulthood.* http://www.pewsocialtrends.org/2014/03/07/millennials-in-adulthood/. Accessed January 11, 2015.

Pew Research Center. (2013). *A rising share of young adults live in their parents' home.* http://www.pewsocialtrends.org/2013/08/01/a-rising-share-of-young-adults-live-in-their-parents-home/. Accessed June 3, 2015.

Pew Research Center. (2012). *Young, underemployed, and optimistic: Coming of age, slowly, in a touch economy.* http://www.pewsocialtrends.org/files/2012/02/young-underemployed-and-optimistic.pdf. Accessed October 8, 2014.

Ritzer, G., & Stepnisky, J. (2013). *Contemporary Sociological Theory and Its Classical Roots: The Basics.* 4th ed. New York, NY: McGraw-Hill.

The Project on Student Debt. (2015). *Student debt and the class of 2014.* http://ticas.org/sites/default/files/pub_files/classof2014.pdf. Accessed June 16, 2017.

Samuel, L. (2012). *The American dream: A cultural history.* Syracuse, NY: Syracuse University Press.

Sandstrom, K., Martin, D., & Fine, G. (2010). *Symbols, selves, and social reality: A symbolic interactionist approach to social psychology and sociology.* 3rd ed. New York, NY: Oxford University Press.

Seidman, S. (1994). *Contested knowledge.* Cambridge, MA: Blackwell Publishers.

Sernau, S. (2017). *Social inequality in a global age.* Thousand Oaks, CA: Sage Publications.

Silva, J. (2014). Slight Expectations: Making sense of the "me me me" generation. *Sociology Compass,* 8(12), 1388–1397.

Sternberg, R. (2013, June 17). Giving employers what they don't really want. *The Chronicle of Higher Education.*

Schwarz, A. (2015). More college freshman report having felt depressed. *The New York Times.* http://www.nytimes.com/2015/02/05/us/more-college-freshmen-report-having-felt-depressed.html?emc=eta1&_r=0. Accessed March 15, 2015.

The boomerang kids speak. (2015). *The New York Times Magazine.* http://www.nytimes.com/interactive/2014/06/22/magazine/100000002949128.mobile.html?_r=0. Accessed June 25, 2014.

United States Census Bureau. (2017). *Residential vacancies and homeownership, second quarter 2017.* https://www.census.gov/housing/hvs/files/currenthvspress.pdf. Accessed October 7, 2017.